I dedicate this compendium to

because

Me

A COMPENDIUM

This book is all about

Sam

(my name)

Date

I'd like to
wear this
every day.

These are my favorite socks.

This is my favorite thing to say.

boul fart~~s~~

← fish food

← mint chocolate chip

← chocalate

These are my top three ice cream flavors.

This is the
best song ever.

title: the hamilton
soundtrack

by: Lin manwel/l
miranda

This is what my hair looks like.

Where I'd love to visit.

This is the funniest joke I know.

I know fill it in
many your one
and
funny Hell
ones ↑ ^your knok
I hope friends. pok

Har har!

Hee hee!

Ha!

Ho hoho!

These are the things I like in my sandwich.

I Do not like sand wens boor I like Burgs but no ches

If I could
have any
pet, it would
be a _giraffe or Dragon._

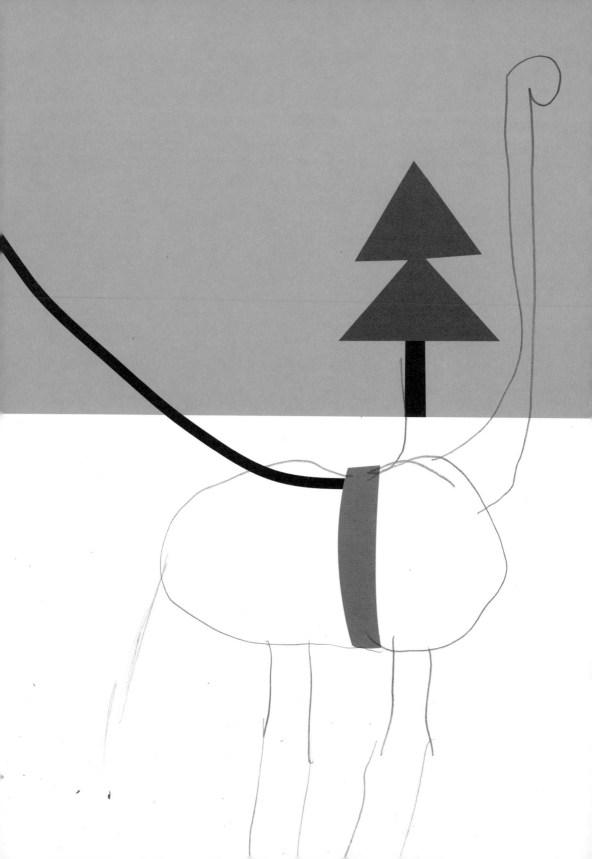

These are the awards I would like to give out.

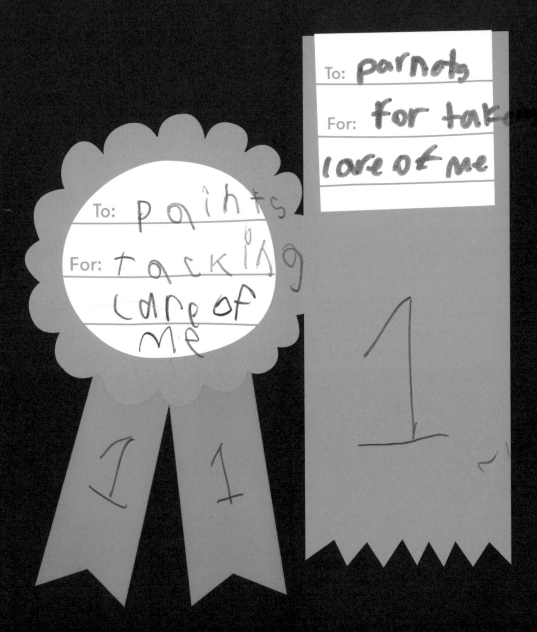

To: paihts
For: tacking care of me

To: parnots
For: for tak care of me

To: my freinds

For: Being Be my

side when I

need them

Love

1

I think this is the best book.

land of storys

and wings of fire
and percey Jackson

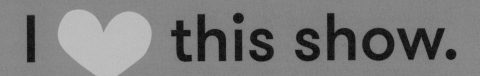

I ♥ this show.

Star streak
nailed it,
floor is lava,
He gose wrons
show

Rate each kind of weather.

Sunny

Snow

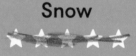

Cloudy

Rain

Freezing

Tornado

★★★★★

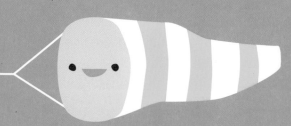

Windy

Thunderstorm

Hot

★

Fog

★★★

This shape reminds me of

Jelly fish

I think this
looks like

Some things that fit in my hand.

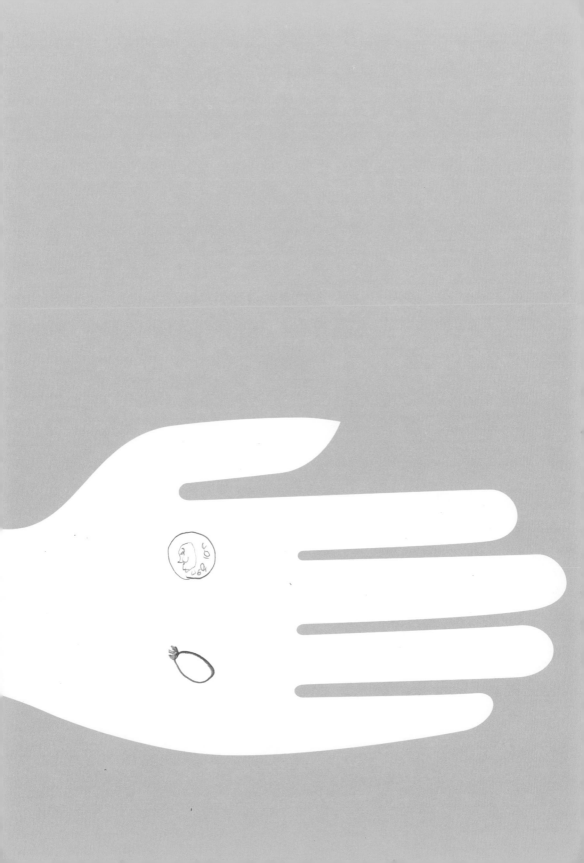

My favorite color is

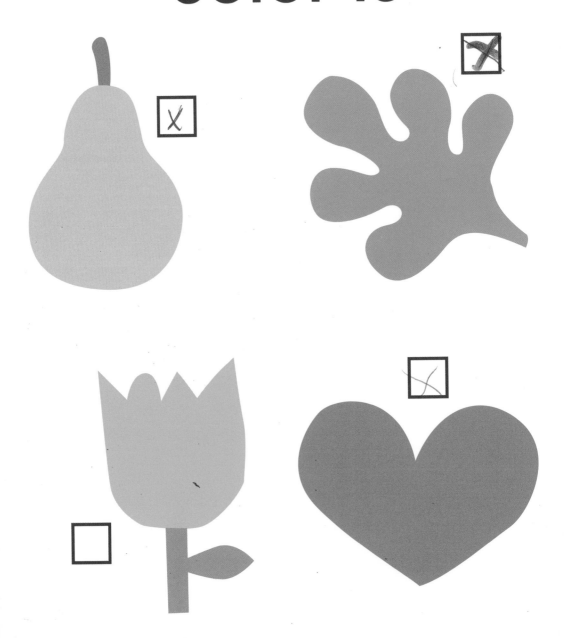

How I looked as a baby.

How I look today.

How I'll look when I'm fifty.

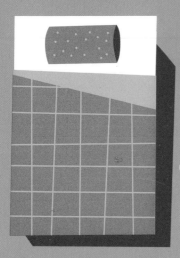

Number of steps
from my bed

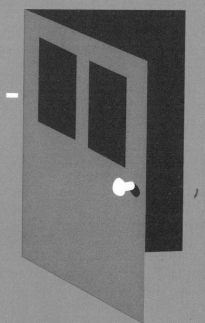

to the front door.

If I had a
band, it
would
be called

These are the things in my brain.

If I had a castle
this would
be my flag.

If I had a shop, it would be called

A BCo

Petl

and I would sell

PE ⊕ SUP lI5e

It would look like this.

This is what
I would look like
if I were a snake.

This is my room.

This is the room
of my dreams.

This is when I wake up.

This is when I go to bed.

I am <u>53 $\frac{1}{2}$</u> inches tall.

When I play Top Secret Spy, I go by the code name

Agent ~~gadget~~ .

If I were an underwater creature, this is what I would be.

If I were going to outer space, this is what I would pack.

This is my favorite thing to do inside.

This is my favorite thing to do outside.

soccer

climtrees

friends

family

Yum! This is my favorite dinner...

...and my least favorite. Blech!

Something I love
that starts with the letter L.

And one thing
I'm not so crazy about.

My birthday is on

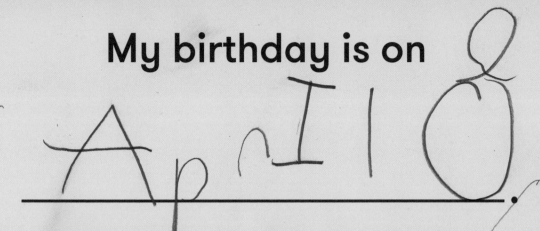

April 8.

This is how I'd decorate my cake.

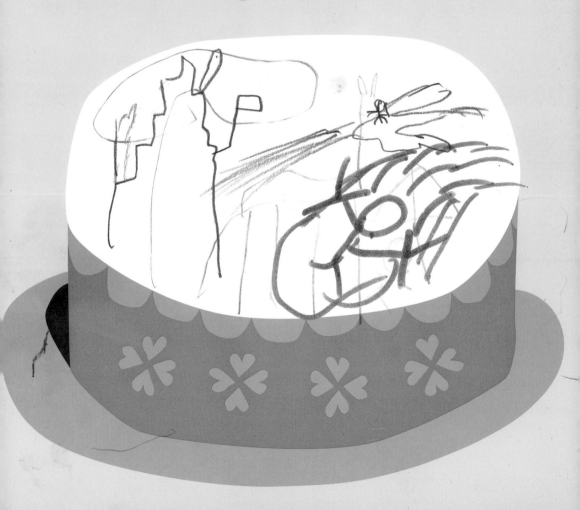

What I wish was inside my refrigerator.

food

cheesy

This is a
bear cub's paw.

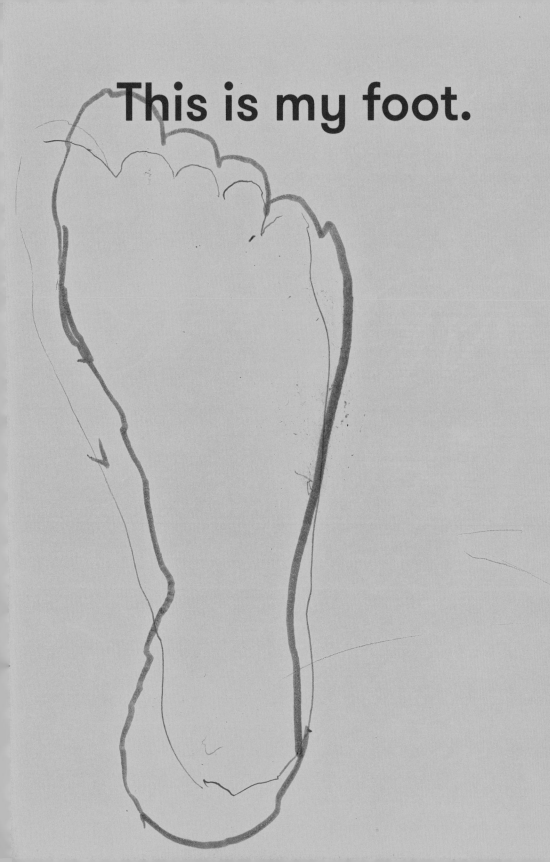

This is my foot.

This is how I feel about

lightning

lizards

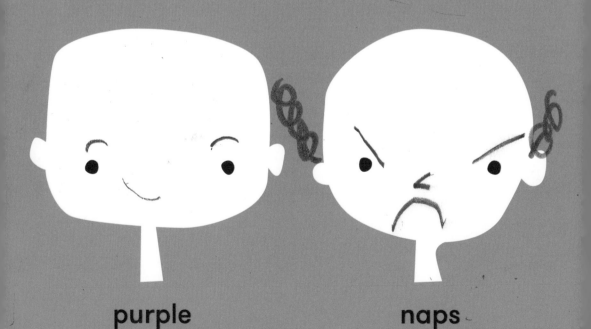

purple

naps

pickles

green shoes

stars

pirates

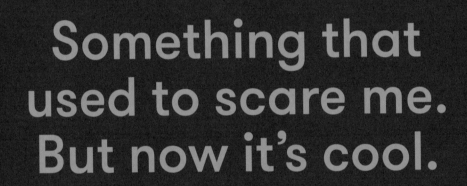

Something that used to scare me. But now it's cool.

dark

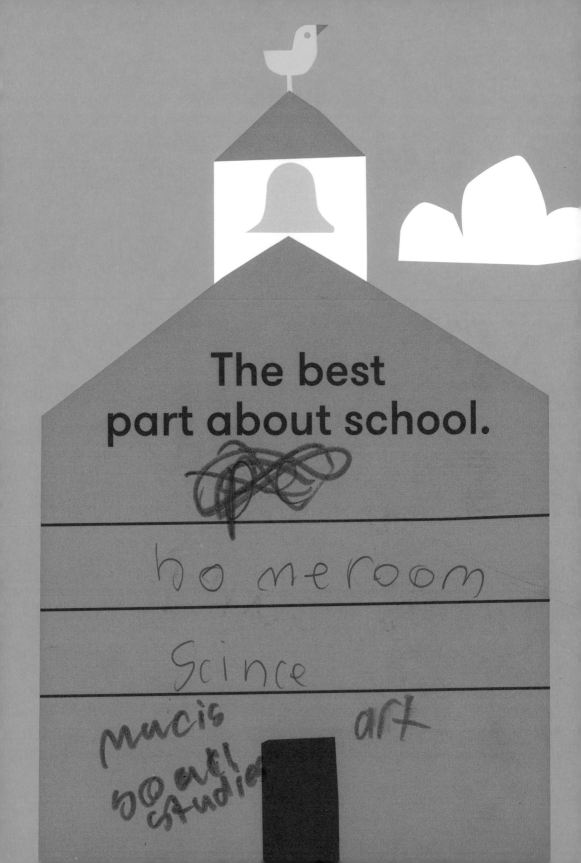

The best
part about school.

ho me room

Scince

mucis   art

yoga
studio

I am a chiken

This is me doing my signature dance move.

If I had a robot, I'd program it to

//:enter_data:

step_01: _____ tell Jokes _____

step_02: _____ help things _____

step_03: _____ play _____

//:run_program

If I were a dinosaur, I'd be a

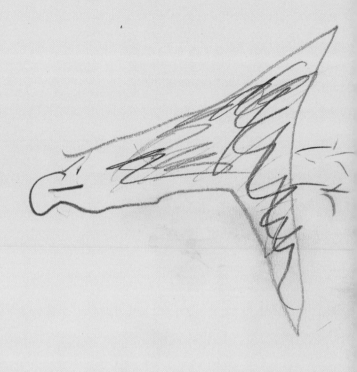

tarata++

I have ▮▮▮▮ teeth.

See?

My
favorite
shoes.

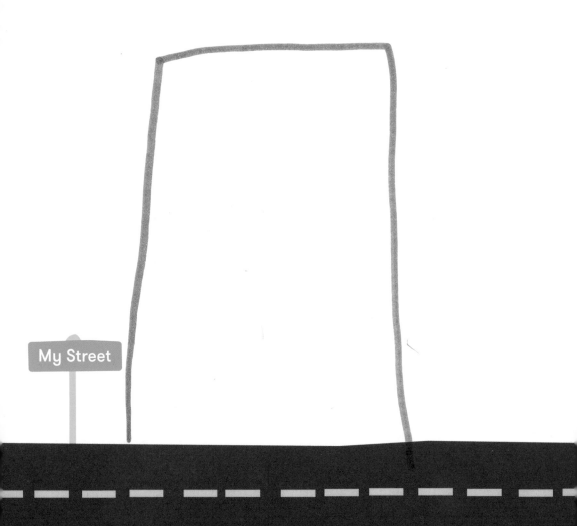

My Street

The best part of
my neighborhood.

my house

My Family

When my family is together, we like to

look

play games

loud

tickl!

LoWe

Sometimes we

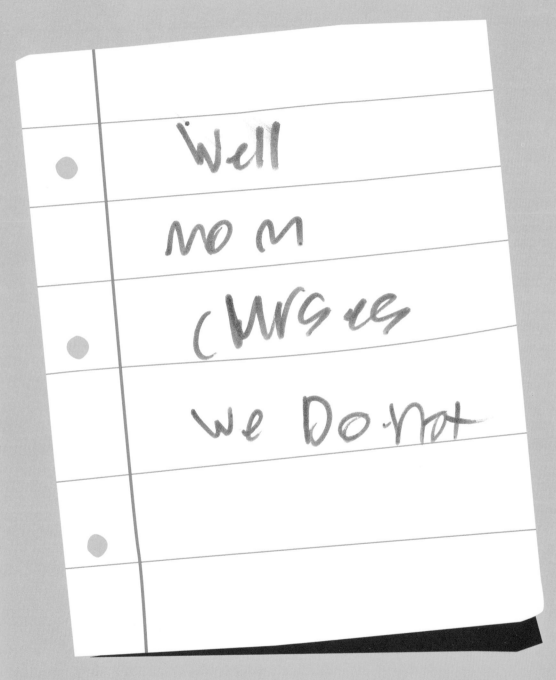

(Yes, really!)

This is

what I'll be

doing when

I grow up

The
Future!

Slaone

These are my best buddies.

Charrlote

Audrey

Lucia

This is my favorite thing to do at the park.

**When I was a baby,
I loved to**

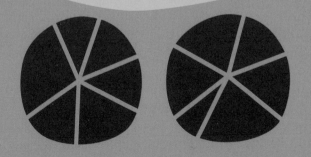

eat aDrink
Soighle run tond

Number of times I can say

fiddly tiddly tink achoo

fast, without laughing: __12__

I cheer for
this team.

These are my favorite fruits.

The best hiding place.

Shhh.

My favorite holiday.

how ween

~~my birthday~~

Number of
jumping jacks
I can do before
I get tired:

_____

Here are some things I have that are round.

This is a map
of where I live.

Home

This is what I'd put in a treasure chest.

This is my favorite tree.

This is how big my hand is.

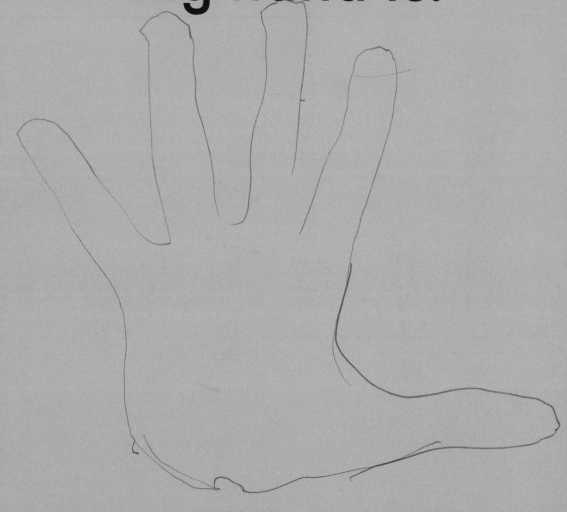

These are the
stickers I'd
put on my
skateboard.

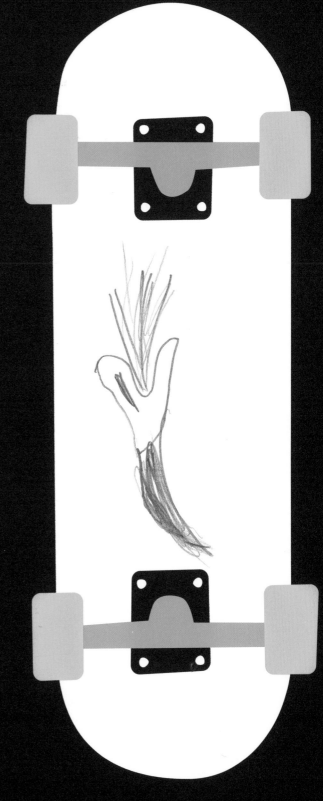

A good name for this bird is

Hello
my name is

Owen

world's best
toy

rodot